WHICH HAT TODAY?

Margaret Ballinger and Rachel Gosset
illustrated by Janet Wolf

ISBN 0-439-14698-4

Copyright © 1996 by Scholastic Australia Pty Limited. All rights reserved.
Published by Scholastic Inc., 555 Broadway, New York, NY 10012,
by arrangement with Scholastic Australia Pty Limited.
SCHOLASTIC and associated logos are trademarks and/or registered
trademarks of Scholastic Inc.

12 11 10 9 8 7 6 5 4 3 2 1   9/9 0 1 2 3 4/0
Printed in the U.S.A.   08
First Scholastic printing, September 1999

SCHOLASTIC INC.
New York   Toronto   London   Auckland   Sydney
Mexico City   New Delhi   Hong Kong

Which hat will I wear today?

rainy

windy

sunny

cold

Which hat will I wear today?
It's a rainy day.
This is the hat I'll wear today.

Which hat will I wear today?
It's a sunny day.
This is the hat I'll wear today.

Which hat will I wear today?
It's a windy day.
This is the hat I'll wear today.

Which hat will I wear today?
It's a cold day.
This is the hat I'll wear today.

Which hat will I wear today?
It's my birthday.
This is the hat I'll wear today.